MW00880571

How to Beat a Narcissist:
99 Toxic and Gaslighting Phrases Explained

Kristen Thrasher
Dominique Fruchtman

© **Copyright Kristen Thrasher 2023 - All rights reserved.**

The content contained within this book may not be reproduced, duplicated or transmitted without direct written permission from the author or the publisher. Under no circumstances will any blame or legal responsibility be held against the publisher, or author, for any damages, reparation, or monetary loss due to the information contained within this book. Either directly or indirectly. You are responsible for your own choices, actions, and results.

<u>Legal Notice:</u>

This book is copyright protected. This book is only for personal use. You cannot amend, distribute, sell, use, quote or paraphrase any part, or the content within this book, without the consent of the author or publisher.

<u>Disclaimer Notice:</u>

Please note the information contained within this document is for educational and entertainment purposes only. All effort has been executed to present accurate, up-to-date, and reliable, complete information. No warranties of any kind are declared or implied. Readers acknowledge that the author is not engaging in the rendering of legal, financial, medical, or professional advice. The content within this book has been derived from various sources. Please consult a licensed professional before attempting any techniques outlined in this book.

By reading this document, the reader agrees that under no circumstances is the author responsible for any losses, direct or indirect, which are incurred as a result of the use of the information contained within this document, including, but not limited to, — errors, omissions, or inaccuracies.

Table of Contents

Introduction

❧ *Every time I voiced my opinion, my ex would quickly shut me down, saying, "I'm smarter than you are, so you need to listen to me." His arrogance knew no bounds. I felt like a scolded child, and it left me feeling belittled and silenced. His need for control was stifling me, and I knew I had to find a way out.*

In the realm of human psychology, narcissists occupy a unique position. Parading a high sense of self-importance, they relentlessly seek admiration and validation. To the world, they present an image of extreme confidence, but paradoxically, they harbor a vulnerable, brittle and low self-esteem beneath their veneer of grandiosity.

Narcissists, ingrained with remarkable cunning, artfully craft a charismatic image, leveraging it to bend reality to their will. But don't be fooled! Hiding right behind that alluring façade, they are emotionally abusive, rooted in a deep-seated insecurity.

The Diagnostic and Statistical Manual of Mental Disorders requires at least five out of the following nine criteria for a clinical narcissism diagnosis:

1. Preoccupation with fantasies of power, unlimited success, beauty, brilliance, or ideal love
2. Need for excessive admiration
3. Lack of empathy
4. Demonstration of arrogant and haughty behaviors or attitudes
5. Sense of entitlement
6. Grandiose sense of self-importance
7. The belief that they are special and unique and can only be understood by, or should associate with, other special or high-status people or institutions
8. Envy of others or a belief that others are envious of them
9. Interpersonally exploitative behavior

Engaging in arguments fuels the narcissist. They use contention as a medium to exert control over others and bolster their power and sense of self-importance. They thrive on victory, deliberately sparking conflicts, leaving those entangled with them drained, defeated and confused.

Their relentless pursuit of triumph transcends boundaries, manipulating conversations in their favor.

Navigating a narcissist's combative style is like deciphering a complex code.

With expert manipulation, they make you buy into their narrative, gaining dominance, regardless of your intelligence or wisdom. Don't blame yourself if you've been reeled into their control. They are pros at this. But they are also cons.

Narcissists are masters of veiled insults, stockpiling an arsenal of cunning phrases to be unleashed when they are ready to strike.

Their aim is to absolve themselves of any fault, shifting it onto you using manipulation, defensiveness, mockery, blame-shifting, and gaslighting.

In this book, we dissect each form of abuse, delving into the narcissist's verbal ammunition, and more importantly, equipping you with 20 retorts to halt their attacks.

Having grappled with narcissistic altercations firsthand, I understand the hardship and frustration of these twisted interactions. Narcissists never surrender, rarely admit their errors, and stash an arsenal of abusive and manipulative tactics, casting *you* as the argument's instigator.

By the end of this journey, you'll comprehend the most common abusive phrases, discerning their real meaning and the narcissist's motivations. With your newfound knowledge, you'll be ready to dodge their advances and stop confrontations cold, all with minimal stress, preserving your dignity as you disengage from the narcissist in your life.

I'm including a number of personal stories in each section of this book. It's important for you to know that you are not alone, and that others have come out intact after a tumultuous and toxic relationship with a narcissist. Some of these stories belong to me, while others come from stories I've heard in support groups such as CoDA (Co-Dependents Anonymous) at coda.org and narcissistabusesupport.com. The stories will be identified by a fleur-de-lis like this: ⚜

⚜ *When I confronted my fiance about his inappropriate behavior at my birthday party, he looked me dead in the eye and said, "I have no idea what you're talking about. That never happened." His denial of reality was shocking. It was like he made me question my own sanity, to make me feel like the irrational one.*

Chapter 1: 21 Manipulation Phrases

❧ Each time I tried to break up with Jake, he'd counter with, "I am the best thing that ever happened to you." It was a chilling statement, making me feel isolated and like I was unworthy of love or understanding from others. It made leaving feel impossible.

The narcissist's preferred form of emotional abuse is manipulation, plain and simple. Twisting the truth is their devious strategy to control and influence you during a disagreement. It serves a dual purpose: to fulfill their cravings for attention and bend the situation to their will.

Narcissists ruthlessly chase their 'narcissistic supply' in a relentless quest for admiration, power, and attention. This unyielding pursuit, fueling their ego, enables them to feel significant and appreciated.

Within the maze of narcissistic conversation, several manipulation phrases stand out as tried and tested weapons. This chapter will dissect the 21 most prominent manipulation phrases, revealing their true purpose in the narcissist's verbal warfare.

1. **"I'm not going to do anything that could upset you."**

This is what a narcissist will claim. But you know it couldn't be further from the truth. This deceptive phrase aims to foster trust in you, making it easier for them to manipulate and control.

2. **"You have trust issues."**

You may or may not have trust issues, but that isn't the point. One common trait all narcissists have in common is a lack of empathy. A narcissist will use this phrase because they don't understand why you don't trust them. A narcissist believes that if someone does something wrong, they are a bad person - and therefore, untrustworthy.

This is the narcissist's attempt to sidestep their lack of empathy and shift the blame on your perceived trust issues, clouding your judgment.

3. **"We are perfect together."**

A classic during the love-bombing phase, this phrase is a bait-and-switch tactic aimed at drawing you in, only for their intentions to change swiftly.

This is the phase at the beginning of a relationship where a narcissist goes overboard trying to show their love for you. A narcissist doesn't say this because they honestly believe the two of you are perfect together. Instead, the narcissist wants to gain your attention, and they need it for their "narcissistic supply".

4. **"I love you more than anything."**
This phrase is also used during the love-bombing phase. A narcissist knows how you feel about them, so they will give you what you need the most - to hear the confession of true love for you. Capitalizing on your emotions, this phrase manipulates your affection for them, making you susceptible to their demands.

5. **"If you do that I won't like you anymore."**
A prime example of emotional blackmailing, this phrase coerces you into proving your love, leaving no room for disagreement or independent thought. They strive to strip you of your independence and freedom, as these elements trigger their insecurities and threats. For a narcissist, the manipulation of your emotions becomes simpler when they can convince you that your happiness is reliant on their affection. They deploy this phrase out of an inability to tolerate any hint of rejection. Their expectation is not just your compliance but your unquestioning obedience, deterring you from doubting or challenging their words or actions.

6. **"You are too sensitive."**

A strategy to trivialize your feelings, this phrase blames you for the issues at hand and further damages your self-esteem. A person grappling with low self-esteem often becomes the prime target for a narcissist. Never owning up to their behavior or actions, a narcissist lives under the delusion that they can never be at fault. They resort to belittling your emotions, accusing you of overreacting or being overly sensitive. Such a tactic serves to further erode your already fragile self-esteem, undermining your mental well-being. When they label you as "too sensitive," it's essentially their way of denying their own culpability in the issue at hand.

7. **"I am the best thing that ever happened to you."**

Asserting their superiority, the narcissist wants you to fear losing them. They harbor an excessively high regard for themselves and a profound sense of entitlement. Their strategy involves making you believe they're the best thing that ever happened to you, instilling in you a fear of losing them.

8. **"Everyone else thinks the same way" or "No one else thinks that."**

By making you question your views, these phrases manipulate you into conforming to their narrative. In deploying either of these manipulative phrases, a narcissist is striving to make you believe that you're "the weirdo" and that your opinion stands in stark contrast to "the rest of the world". That hyperbole alone is a red flag that illustrates their attempt to invalidate your perspective solely on the basis that it diverges from everyone else's. The manipulative tactic here is that if you are the lone advocate for a viewpoint, it must inherently be flawed.

9. "We compliment each other perfectly."

This sly phrase is employed as a ruse to persuade you that you and the narcissist form an "ideal pair" and that your place is with them, fueling their fear of abandonment. A narcissist resorts to this assertion during disputes, driven by their fear of abandonment. They feel a pressing need to implant in your mind that you're destined to be together, dissuading you from contemplating a departure.

10. "I'm only doing this because I love you."

A narcissist continually endeavors to rationalize their poor treatment of you. To justify their mistreatment, this phrase conceals the exploitative and controlling nature behind a façade of affection. They convince themselves that it's acceptable (at times, and for effect) for them to display insecurity or jealousy, citing their "love" for you as the reason. They use phrases like, "I have your best interests at heart" or "I'm only doing this because I love you". However, in reality, these words are merely veils; it means the narcissist is exercising control and exploitation over you and might even mean that you're a little too close to seeing through them.

11. "Nobody likes you - everyone laughs behind your back."

This phrase is a ploy to isolate you and prevent others from revealing their narcissistic traits. In truth, a narcissist engages this phrase as a tactic to obstruct your interactions with anyone who might alert you to the fact that you're entangled in a relationship with a toxic person. Again, you're getting too close to unveiling the truth. They are aware that you're in denial and unable to fully acknowledge the extent of the abuse you're enduring at their hands. The narcissist doesn't want anyone (including this book) to enlighten you, driven by the fear that such revelations might cause you to leave.

12. "I'm the best you'll ever have."

This phrase reinforces their self-perception of superiority and their fear of being insufficient. It's also among the most frequently used by a narcissist, firmly believing that they are the epitome of an ideal romantic partner. They hold themselves in such delusional and highly favorable regard, they are driven by the urge to uphold their overly positive self-images. As a result, a narcissist might appear as if they have lowered their standards to be with you, or that you're undeserving of a relationship with them. However, don't be deceived by the narcissist's illusion! By using this phrase, a narcissist is, in fact, revealing their fear that they are not good enough for you, and that you may swiftly discern this unless they convince you otherwise.

13. **"It's always something with you."**
Narcissists use this phrase as a diversionary tactic to evade conversations they'd rather avoid. The subject matter could be anything; regardless of its relevance or gravity, they dismiss it. They employ this tactic simply to sidestep issues that are not in their favor, promote them in some way or paint them in a less-than-positive light. But the stark reality is that the problem rarely stems from you.

14. **"You pissed me off - that's why I said all those mean things to you."**
"You made me do this" is among a narcissist's top manipulative statements. Shifting the blame for their abusive behavior onto you, this phrase excuses their inability to

manage their anger. They use it as an excuse to rationalize all their actions, pointing a finger at you for instigating their abusive and manipulative behavior. Bizarrely, the narcissist convinces themselves that you uniquely elicit their worst side, whereas everyone else apparently draws out the best in them. By using this phrase, a narcissist is admitting their inability to manage their anger issues, choosing instead to offload that guilt onto you.

15. **"Others think I'm a pretty great person. Too bad you don't."**

The narcissist weaponizes their supposed perfection to invalidate your complaints. This statement clearly suggests that you are likely dealing with a narcissist, given their conviction in their own perfection and flawlessness. Accordingly, they assume everyone else shares the same perception of their perfection. The remaining task for them is to persuade you of their perfection. In short, a narcissist employs this phrase as a tool to manipulate you into viewing them flawlessly, thereby implying that they could not possibly be at fault in any disagreement.

16. **"You have to pick a side."**

This phrase employed by a narcissist is a clever ploy for emotional blackmail to ensure you always choose them over everyone else.

The narcissist demands your unwavering loyalty, as if they were the only person left on Earth with whom you could share the rest of your life. The narcissist might react with discomfort (or even shun you) if you fail to consistently prioritize them over all others in your life. What this phrase truly conveys is their demand for you to love them more than anyone else, to always select them, to always side with them. It's their way of asserting that they should be the paramount figure in your life.

17. "I used to think you were a good person."

This is another narcissistic phrase that is a prime example of manipulation combined with blame-shifting designed to pull you down to their level. A narcissist actually means that they aren't anywhere close to becoming the person they aspire to be, so they will use everything in their toolbox to drag you down with them. Other common phrases a narcissist will use similar to this one include, "How can you, of all people, say that?", "I am so disappointed in you", and "I didn't expect this from you".

18. "You'll never find anyone as good as me."

The phrase is strikingly similar to the #12, "I'm the best you'll ever have." By weaponizing this remark, a narcissist is working to convince you that they truly are the best romantic partner you have ever or could ever have. This belief, deeply rooted in their perpetual conviction of superiority, further amplifies their exaggerated sense of self-importance.

19. "No wonder you have so few friends."

A narcissist will resort to this phrase when they unearth something personal or unconventional about you that triggers your insecurities. Suppose they learn that you abstain from alcohol due to a history of alcoholism in your family. Rather than applauding your resilience and providing support, they critique and alienate you. Essentially, a narcissist employs this phrase to isolate you, leading you to believe that they are the only ones tolerant enough to accept your perceived peculiarity.

20. "Let's just both forgive and forget."

A narcissist prefers to suggest mutual forgiveness and forgetfulness, avoiding any admission of their mistake that necessitates an apology. However, it's important to remember that *forgiveness* doesn't equate to *reconciliation*. While you might forgive a narcissist, maintaining your personal boundaries remains crucial.

21. "It's my way or the highway."

A narcissist is firmly convinced that only their solution to a problem is the right one! They see things in black and white - it's either their way, or it's unquestionably incorrect. By employing this phrase as a form of emotional blackmail, a narcissist seeks to assert complete control over you.

⚜ *Reflecting on my marriage to my ex-husband, I still remember how often he labeled me as "too sensitive" or claimed there was "always something" bothering me. His constant assertions that I was "impossible to please" became a running theme in our relationship, and the irony is, it was so far from the truth.*

He had a knack for twisting even the simplest of conversations, such as discussing household chores or dinner plans, into full-blown arguments. Instead of just taking out the heavy trash cans to the curb like every other husband on our block (they were way too heavy for me because I'm very petite), he painted himself as the selfless provider, working ceaselessly to support our family, showering me with "nice things" as if that was a currency for love and respect.

Yet, he deemed any request or disagreement from me as an insatiable demand. His favorite refrain was, "No matter what I do, you are never satisfied." He'd persistently belittle my feelings, making me feel as though I was a bottomless pit of needs and complaints.

In hindsight, I realize his accusations were just a form of deflection, a way to avoid taking responsibility for his actions. If there was ever a task he didn't want to do, or a topic he wanted to evade, he'd retaliate by claiming that nobody could ever make me happy. He even had the audacity to suggest I should be grateful he puts up with me, as nobody else would tolerate my supposed demands.

Looking back, I see now that I was not the problem - he was.

Chapter 2: 19 Defensive Phrases

❧ *I was pouring my heart out to my girlfriend by making myself vulnerable for the first time in ages. What a huge mistake. I was calmly expressing my fears and anxieties when she dismissed me with a scornful head shake. "You're just too emotional." I felt invalidated, my feelings discarded like they were nothing. It was heartbreaking to realize that the person I loved had so little empathy for me. It's still hard for me to be honest about my feelings because of how deeply this hurt me.*

A narcissist is dazzling, magnetic, captivating, charming, and even beguiling at the beginning of a relationship. However, as the relationship progresses and the initial enchantment phase concludes, their demeanor abruptly switches to aggressive, competitive, obnoxious, vindictive, entitled, detached, exploitative, selfish, cruel, and arrogant.

While it's effortless to be drawn to their charming and courteous demeanor, their darker side, when unveiled, can leave you emotionally shattered. This shift typically begins when their defensive mechanisms start to surface.

The defensive strategies employed by a narcissist to shield their vulnerabilities make maintaining a relationship exceedingly challenging. As narcissists rarely, if ever, believe they are in the wrong, they can become excessively defensive at the slightest hint of criticism. This propensity is evident in many of the defensive phrases they often resort to during a disagreement.

In this chapter, we will delve into 19 of the most common defensive phrases a narcissist tends to use during a confrontation

1. **"Let's concentrate on the positive aspects."**

   This manipulative phrase is employed by a narcissist to divert attention away from the problematic situation, particularly when they've acted in an abusive or hurtful manner. This defensive statement seeks to project an image of a trouble-free relationship, despite the tangible issues that exist. The use of this phrase can be incredibly damaging, as it leaves you feeling impotent. It fosters a disconcerting realization that nothing will improve unless action is taken.

2. **"You're behaving badly."**

   This statement is a typical example of a defense tactic called projective identification, and is frequently employed by narcissists. In short, a narcissist transfers their emotions onto someone else to avoid dealing with them. Especially when their actions are challenged or they are accused of wrongdoing, a narcissist will invariably seek to shift the blame from them to you.

3. **"I am already going through so much - thanks for making it worse."**

     The resort to self-pity is another characteristic defensive maneuver used by narcissists. Phrases like "I am in so much pain", "You know how depressed I am", or "My life is so difficult right now" frequently surface in their arguments. The reason for this is rooted in their firm belief that their issues are graver than anyone else's owing to their exaggerated sense of self-importance. As a result, they expect you to give in and let them win the argument, using their personal troubles as a persuasive tactic.

4. **"You keep bringing up the past."**

     This defensive phrase is commonly used by narcissists to redirect blame back towards you. When confronted with their own wrongdoing, a narcissist would rather suggest that you're the one responsible for granting them forgiveness for their misdeeds. If they've engaged in behaviors that provoke you (like dishonesty or infidelity), they'll blame you for being incapable of "forgiving and forgetting" to move past the issue, thereby skewing the situation to make it seem like you're the one at fault.

5. **"You are way too emotional."**

This statement is a clear indicator of a narcissist's inability to empathize with others. The underlying aim is to frame your emotional response as a sign of frailty or a source of embarrassment. Despite your reactions being completely valid, this phrase is designed to manipulate you into feeling differently. A narcissist is aware that using inflammatory language will discourage you from freely expressing your emotions in the future, achieving their ultimate objective of control.

6. **"We don't need anyone else."**

A narcissist will use this phrase to ensure your unwavering loyalty and obedience. If you're being reprimanded by a narcissist for socializing with others, keep in mind that their aim is to distance you from friends and family and make you solely reliant on them. What a narcissist really implies when using this phrase is their desire for exclusive possession of you, without the necessity of competing for your attention or time.

7. **"I do so much for you."**

A narcissist holds the conviction that their past kind deeds, generally during the love-bombing stage, should always be kept top of mind regardless of how much time has passed. They see their past benevolence like a bank account, ready to be drawn upon whenever they need to look good. Regardless of the time gap since their last compliment or gift, they maintain the notion that you are eternally in their debt.

8. **"You're just looking for reasons to fight with me."**

Every time you try to express your feelings or explain why you are upset, a narcissist will manage to make you feel like you've done something drastically wrong. They have a knack for devaluing your emotions, making it seem as if your only intention is to upset them. They know they're in denial, and by using this phrase, they're essentially telling you that they don't need a reality check.

9. **"That's stupid."**

Don't allow a narcissist's belittling comments about your ideas or behaviors undermine your self-worth. It's actually the narcissist who is lacking in discernment. Disparaging and superior statements like these erode your self-confidence, making you feel marginalized yet somehow lucky to receive their attention.

10. **"How dare you accuse me of doing that!"**

Translated: "You're the real bully here" is indeed a form of DARVO, a psychological manipulation tactic often used by narcissists to deflect blame and responsibility. Here's a breakdown of DARVO:

A. Deny: The narcissist denies the wrongdoing, making you question your perception of the reality or event.
B. Attack: The narcissist attacks you, usually with personal insults or attempts to discredit you. This can destabilize you emotionally and mentally, making it harder for you to maintain your perspective.
C. Reverse Victim and Offender: The narcissist portrays themselves as the victim and you as the offender, further muddying your perception of the situation.

Narcissists are masters at twisting reality in their favor and will use a multitude of manipulation tactics to avoid taking responsibility for their actions. They're adept at turning situations around to make themselves appear as the victim, regardless of their actions. The goal of using such a phrase is to make you second-guess your reality, your perceptions, and even your worth.

Recognizing these patterns is crucial for maintaining your sanity and emotional health. Standing up to such manipulation often requires professional support and the development of strong boundaries. It's also important to rely on trusted friends, family, or support groups to validate your experiences and feelings.

11. "You always take everything the wrong way."

Amazing! It's your fault again somehow. It's enough to make you wonder why someone so amazing would tolerate a loser like you. Also known as, "You misunderstood me" is a common deflection tactic used by a narcissist. When they say this, they are again shifting the blame for a miscommunication or misunderstanding onto you, rather than accepting that they may have said something hurtful, inappropriate, or simply wrong. This strategy serves a dual purpose: it allows the narcissist to evade responsibility for their words and actions, and it works to continue to undermine your confidence in your own perceptions and judgment, a form of gaslighting.

While it's true that misunderstandings can occur in any relationship, a pattern of "you misunderstood me" can be a red flag, especially if the narcissist never seems to take responsibility for their part in these misunderstandings.

In response to this tactic, you can ask for clarification. However, be prepared for more deflection, denial, or even aggression. Remember, with narcissists, the goal is often to control and dominate the narrative, not to reach a shared understanding or resolution.

It's critically important to trust your *own* perceptions and feelings. If someone repeatedly makes you feel disrespected, dismissed, or confused, it's worth considering whether the relationship is healthy and respectful.

12. "I'm smarter than you, so you should listen to me."

It's astounding that anyone would have the audacity to utter such a statement, isn't it? Yet, it's perfectly in character for a narcissist. Remember that they are the sole believer in their intellectual superiority. Do not let them persuade you into thinking this is a *fact*. The underlying motive for this statement is a pathetic attempt to convince you to abandon your perspectives, enabling the narcissist to seize control. Ultimately, their aim is always about gaining supremacy over you and the situation at hand.

13. "You are so moody, I can't keep up with all of your mood swings!"

Once again, the narcissist is deploying their blame-shifting tactic to make you the culprit for the conflict. They will resort to any means necessary to validate their point. Their primary aim is to establish you as the cause. They might even resort to labeling you as 'moody,' believing that this at least provides a reason for the dispute.

14. "This is how you repay me for all I've done for you?"

This is one of the most prevalent phrases a narcissist will use during a conflict. You might also hear, "I've done so much for you, but you never show any gratitude." A narcissist meticulously catalogs every good deed they perform for you because they anticipate a reciprocal act in the future. They operate under the assumption that you are indebted to them due to their acts of kindness, and as such, they should be entitled to prevail in every disagreement.

15. "That never happened."

It's difficult for a narcissist to take accountability for their actions because, according to research, a narcissist isn't as prone to guilt as others are. You should never accuse a narcissist of anything if you don't have actual hard evidence or proof to back up your claims because a narcissist will deny it, every single time. They will say it never happened or you are making it up in your head. A narcissist will come up with anything in order to avoid having to take responsibility for their actions. Some of the most common phrases a narcissist uses include, "I never said that", and "Your evidence doesn't prove anything". A narcissist uses phrases like these when they actually know they are guilty, but choose to continue to outright deny it in order to cause you to doubt yourself.

16. **"You're being unreasonable."**

A narcissist using the phrase is a classic example of gaslighting. They're dismissing your feelings and experiences by painting you as overly emotional or fragile. It is a way of invalidating your experiences, making you feel wrong for having the reactions that you do.

When they say this, they are not just being dismissive, they are manipulating the situation to make themselves appear as the reasonable party, and you as the irrational one. It's a defensive tactic to avoid accountability for their actions. When a narcissist uses this phrase, they're essentially communicating that they don't want to take responsibility for the effects of their behavior, nor do they want to change or compromise. It's an attempt to shift the blame onto you for having a normal emotional response.

Recognizing these manipulative tactics can be a powerful step towards setting boundaries and seeking healthier relationships.

17. "I'm sorry you feel that way."

A narcissist might offer an insincere apology that subtly shifts the blame to your feelings, making it seem as if your reaction is the problem, not their actions. It also hints at a kind of pity, as if to say, "I feel sorry for you for feeling that way." This kind of statement, often disguised as an apology, actually seeks to undermine your experience and feelings. Instead of acknowledging their mistakes, a narcissist uses these phrases to evade responsibility and maintain their self-perception of infallibility. In essence, when a narcissist uses this phrase, they are communicating their unwillingness to acknowledge their harmful actions or take any responsibility for them.

18. "You are always making shit up in your head."

When a narcissist uses this phrase, they're attempting to undermine your perceptions and feelings, casting doubt on your understanding of the situation. This is a form of gaslighting, a manipulative tactic narcissists use to make you question your own memory, judgment, and sanity. It's a method of psychological manipulation to gain more control and dominance in the relationship. By causing you to doubt your own experiences, they divert attention away from their harmful actions and behaviors.

19. "You're just trying to start drama."

Narcissists often use this defensive phrase to discredit your feelings and concerns, framing them as an unnecessary attempt to stir up trouble. Instead of addressing the actual issues at hand, they try to divert the attention and place the blame back on you. The implication here is that your complaints or concerns are not valid, but are rather a dramatic overreaction or fabrication on your part. This is also a gaslighting technique (discussed later) that is designed to make you question the validity of your feelings while the narcissist casts themselves as the "reasonable one" in the situation. The intent behind this phrase is to keep you off balance while skillfully avoiding taking responsibility for their actions.

⚜ *My ex-wife, Sarah, had an uncanny knack for turning any conversation into a lecture about her sacrifices and efforts. Each time I tried to voice a concern or asked for some assistance around the house, she would launch into a monologue detailing her exhaustive to-do list.*

The mornings were spent getting the kids ready and driving them to school, followed by cleaning the house, managing laundry, and planning dinner. The afternoons would be filled with picking up the kids, shuttling them to their after-school activities, and the list went on. It was as if she was heroically tackling these tasks single-handedly for my sake, conveniently forgetting that these were responsibilities she'd shoulder even if I weren't in the picture.

She loved to remind me of her constant sacrifices. "I do so much for you," she'd say, followed by the kicker, "This is how you repay me for everything I've done for you?" I wasn't asking for repayments or scorekeeping. I just wanted open communication, a partnership where we both felt heard and appreciated.

But her story in her mind was clear: She was the long-suffering, tireless worker bee, and I was the ungrateful beneficiary of her ceaseless efforts. And God forbid if I voiced a different perspective - I'd be faced with the full force of her self-proclaimed martyrdom. It was her way of staying in control, avoiding accountability, and always being the one who was 'put upon.'

Chapter 3: 21 Mocking Phrases

⚜ *In an argument about our future together, Rebecca resorted to gaslighting. "Everyone thinks you're wrong," she used to say, as if people were gossiping about me behind my back to her. And as if their opinion had any place in our personal lives! It was such a low blow, and a pretty successful attempt to make me feel isolated and alone.*

A narcissist is nothing if not adaptive, employing a vast array of tactics in any argument. Don't expect them to rely on the same tricks, though; it's not unusual for a narcissist to dip into each category of phrases covered in this book.

Another insidious form of emotional abuse that a narcissist resorts to in an argument is belittlement or mockery. In their relentless pursuit to appear superior, they will do their utmost to make you feel intellectually deficient or unworthy.

Prepare yourself to hear the subsequent 22 phrases, frequently used by narcissists as potent tools of derision, aimed to inflict emotional distress and ridicule during contentious exchanges.

1. **"You look stupid doing that."**

When a narcissist says this, they're banking on your self-esteem being brittle enough to crumble under their words. They're hoping you'll accept their harsh judgment and cease the action they're criticizing. This is merely another facet of their manipulation playbook, designed to ensure they maintain the upper hand.

2. **"It was just a joke."**

A narcissist does a brilliant job downplaying their insults as mere jest when they see you're hurt. However, humor should never be a cover for degradation. Trust your instincts when discerning between a genuine joke and a disguised insult. If their so-called 'joke' was hurtful, don't let their explanation trivialize your feelings. Whether their intent was to jest or not is immaterial - what matters is that you were hurt by their words.

3. **"Here we go again."**

The narcissist says this to paint you as irrational and unyielding, especially when you're seeking resolution for a contentious issue that wasn't resolved completely (or at all) the first time around. It could be about a broken promise, a betrayal, or any hurtful act.

Your quest for a genuine resolution, perhaps even through professional help like therapy, is portrayed as your inability to "let go of the past" and your penchant for "dwelling on old issues". Ignoring the fact that this so-called "old issue" might have occurred just a few weeks ago, they intend to make you feel like you're the one perpetually stirring the pot. This lingering feeling of discontent you have is a direct result of the lack of closure, resolution, or sincere remorse you initially received when the situation first occurred and their denial, deflection or gaslighting brought a swift end to the discussion.

4. **"I have more experience and knowledge than you."**

A narcissist is perpetually convinced of their intellectual superiority over everyone in their orbit. This ingrained belief fuels their assumption that they are naturally entitled to be the decision-makers and the ones in control. With this phrase, a narcissist seeks to fulfill their desires, while simultaneously safeguarding their self-perceived intelligence and authority from any scrutiny or dissent. If you dare to depart from their views or decisions, even slightly, they will belittle you, causing you to feel insignificant and inadequate. Their mantra is unflinchingly clear: it's their way or no way at all.

5. **"Don't cry - you are only trying to manipulate me."**

The insidious nature of emotional abuse leads to its normalization in many relationships. This is especially true when the abuser is a narcissist, whose abuse is often subtle, frequent, and can go unrecognized for an extended period. Many victims do not clearly see the extent of the toxicity they endure daily, which, in turn, delays their extraction from their damaging environments.

A common tactic used by narcissists is making their victims feel weak, especially when they dismissively tell you to stop crying. If you look carefully, they are projecting their insecurities onto you, accusing you of the very behavior they display. When a narcissist tells you to stop expressing your emotions, what they're really saying is they don't want to deal with your feelings. They want to suppress your emotional response to maintain control and avoid any accountability.

6. **"I can't have any negative emotions around you."**

Confrontation unnerves narcissists, leading to reactions that can range from chilling indifference to explosive hysteria. When you stand up to their abusive behavior, they frequently resort to defensive phrases such as that above or, "You make it impossible for me to be myself around you." This statement is a classic diversion tactic. Yet again, the narcissist attempts to shift the blame onto you, making it seem as if your rightful objection to their misconduct is an attack on their personal freedom or identity. In reality, what they are communicating is that they feel constrained because they cannot continue their abusive behavior without facing consequences.

7. "You need to see a therapist."

There is no shame in seeking therapy or needing mental health support, but when a narcissist says this, they twist it into a derogatory statement, weaponizing it to demean and discredit you. Their self-anointed status as an authority allows them to label you as mentally unstable, reinforcing their narrative that *you're* the one with the issue, not them. This way, if you leave them, they can conveniently include you in their dismissive narrative that 'all their exes have been crazy', thereby avoiding any accountability for their actions.

8. "All of my exes have been crazy."

Narcissists have an uncanny knack for painting their ex-partners as deranged individuals. They'll regale you with tales of their 'crazy exes', portraying themselves as victims of these supposedly unstable individuals. They might even cheekily ask, "Does that make me crazy too?" But don't be fooled. This is a calculated move to manipulate your perception of them. By undermining the credibility of their exes beforehand, they're essentially setting the stage to excuse their own past misdeeds. So when you eventually stumble upon questionable actions from their past relationships, you'll chalk it up to the crazy ex and not their provoking behavior.

9. **"There's something wrong with you."**

It's crucial not to buy into this fallacy. The issue lies not with you, but with the narcissist who resorts to these deplorable tactics. These kinds of statements are attempts to undermine your self-confidence and destabilize your mental well-being. Try not to let these statements damage your self-esteem or adversely affect your mental health. Remember, you are not the one at fault. It's their inability to maintain healthy and respectful relationships that is the *real* problem.

10. **"You are making a fool out of yourself by behaving that way."**

A narcissist is perpetually ready to belittle you or make you feel inadequate. One of their favorite techniques is to emphasize your mistakes or inaccuracies, regardless of how trivial they might be. They deploy this tactic as a means to assert their dominance and discourage any opposition or scrutiny of their actions. In essence, the narcissist wants to establish an environment where their decisions and behaviors remain unquestioned, and using this phrase is a key part of their strategy. They want to keep you in a state of self-doubt, thereby reinforcing their control over you.

11. "Relax. It's not that big of a deal."

A narcissist will often make statements along the lines of "It's such a trivial issue; don't exaggerate it." Research has found that a narcissist has a limited self-awareness and a reduced ability to attune to others. This can explain why a narcissist doesn't see their poor behaviors in the same light as you do. By using this phrase, a narcissist will downplay or minimize your distress when they notice you are confronting them.

12. "You're being irrational."

This is a phrase the narcissist will use to make you feel like your feelings are wrong or invalid. However, you must understand that there is actually no such thing as being irrational, only feeling things others don't agree with or understand. You may have a strong suspicion that you are being treated unfairly, but the narcissist will try to convince you that is not the case, regardless of the situation.

13. "I have no idea what you're talking about."

A narcissist is quick to play dumb. In fact, this is often their go-to strategy. Some other examples of this kind of phrase include,

"Where is this coming from?", "What do you mean when you say that?", and "I just don't understand." However, this really means that the narcissist knows exactly what you are talking about - they just have no desire to have a conversation with you about it.

14. "Not everything is about you."

Because a narcissist has such a low self-esteem, they need people to validate and admire them constantly. They have trouble understanding others due to their lack of empathy. They also feel entitled, expect special privileges (that they won't give back in return), and require lots of attention. Therefore, they will use this phrase to remind you that not everything is about you, because it always has to be about them, instead. A narcissist will become defensive if you steal their spotlight, even briefly. If you take the focus away from them, the narcissist will attempt to make you feel embarrassed and guilty. Guilt-tripping in relationships is just another form of abuse. A narcissist will use this phrase as a way to warn you not to steal their thunder.

15. "You're so lucky I put up with you."

A narcissist feels like they are actually doing you a favor simply by being with you, due to their inflated sense of self. The narcissist expects you to feel blessed and grateful that they have chosen to be with and stay with you. The intention behind this phrase is to make you feel completely and utterly worthless. However, when a narcissist uses this phrase they are actually insinuating that they are scared you are starting to pull away from them and might eventually leave them for good.

16. "You need to grow up!"

One of the most common phrases a narcissist uses to mock their victim in an argument is telling you to grow up, or that you are acting like an immature child. A narcissist believes they are mature and you, in contrast, are not. We all know that this is so far from the truth, and in fact, quite the opposite is true. But there is really no point in even trying to argue with a narcissist, as you will never be able to win any argument. A narcissist will claim that everything you say is irrational, as they are the only person in the world who makes any sense or has the right point of view. Ultimately, a narcissist uses this phrase to calm their insecurities by ridiculing you.

17. "Everyone agrees with me."

This manipulative phrase has the added bonus of making you feel isolated, as well as feeling stupid. The narcissist believes you will back down if they can convince you that any reasonable person would agree with them, and begin to question your own reality. It can be hard to see the manipulation in this phrase if you are already having doubts about yourself in this area.

18. "You're crazy."

One of the classic narcissistic argument tactics is calling you "crazy". A narcissist is actually called a "crazy maker" - meaning they are able to establish control over you by making you question your sanity or reality. The narcissist thinks you are acting crazy, when really you have just finally figured out their abusive tendencies and have begun confronting them, which they don't like. This phrase is a classic gaslighting technique that is used to make you doubt your sanity, as well as kill your self-esteem. In using this phrase, a narcissist actually means that they are going to stop listening because they refuse to take responsibility for anything.

19. "Maybe we should end things."

In all reality, the narcissist has absolutely no intention of breaking up with you. But a narcissist is prone to say one thing and do the opposite. They will bring up the topic of ending the relationship with you on a regular basis because they love it when you show signs you are begging them for love. A narcissist loves you to see you become paranoid and freak out. It gives a narcissist a great sense of pleasure to see how scared you are to lose them.

20. **"You always misinterpret what others say."**
A narcissist will use this phrase when they are confronted in order to turn the tables around on you. This causes you to feel bad for ever questioning them. This phrase is really common when you suggest the narcissist has done anything wrong. A narcissist may also say things like, "Why do you always feel like I am attacking you?" or "You always take things the wrong way", or "Not everyone is out to get you".

21. **"I don't know what you want me to say."**
The narcissist is in shock when they use this phrase. This may be said when you are trying to get them to understand your point of view. Or they may not like hearing calm and reasonable questions about their behavior. It is the narcissist's way or prematurely shutting down the conversation. You have brought forth all of your proof or evidence. You have finally cornered them and they still won't give you the satisfaction of admitting they were wrong. Instead, they will refuse to answer you and use this phrase to dismiss your concerns. This phrase is much easier for a narcissist to say

than having to mutter the words you are longing to hear… "I'm sorry".

 ⚜ *I recall a specific instance when my ex-husband, a textbook narcissist, seized an opportunity to belittle me during a friendly game of bowling. It was my first time trying the sport, and instead of supporting me or offering helpful tips, he exploited my inexperience to ridicule me in front of our friends. Every time I bowled a gutter ball or failed to knock down all the pins, he'd loudly proclaim, "Look at how bad she is at this! Sweetheart, I'm going to go ask the manager if they offer trophies for the worst bowler of the month. I wonder why you're forgetting all the advice I gave you?"*

His hurtful comments stung. But even in the midst of the mockery, a part of me wondered if his behavior stemmed from fear - perhaps he was afraid that if I improved, I might outshine him or even become better than him. Or perhaps he merely wanted all the attention to remain focused on him. Regardless of his motives, reflecting on that episode now, I realize just how toxic his behavior was. He didn't hesitate to undermine my confidence in order to inflate his own ego. His intent was to keep me in a constant state of self-doubt and unease, a classic maneuver used by narcissists to maintain control.

Chapter 4: 19 Blame-Shifting Phrases

⚜ *One night, I caught my longtime boyfriend Mike texting romantically with another woman. When I confronted him, his reaction was not what I expected. "You always overreact," he said, as if my feelings of disbelief and betrayal were nothing more than a spoiled child throwing a temper tantrum! He got real calm and "adult-seeming" all of a sudden, like he was trying to show how calm and "rational" he was while I stood there with tears in my eyes, demanding answers. I felt so invalidated, like my reaction - perfectly normal reaction - was just an inconvenience to him. It was crazy and surreal how little he cared about my pain.*

Blame-shifting is a defense mechanism in which a narcissist will avoid accountability for something they did or said by deflecting the blame onto you. Blame-shifting is often used as a response to an accusation or complaint towards the narcissist. It is another emotionally-abusive tactic often employed by narcissists.

Ultimately, the narcissist will find a way to shift the blame back on you and completely take the focus and accountability off of themselves.

Blame-shifting often causes even more conflict in your relationship, because it shuts down all communication between you and the narcissist. It can lead to escalating arguments because you will become frustrated or angry when the blame is shifting you instead of your complaints actually being heard and worked through.

Blame-shifting goes hand-in-hand with emotional abuse. It is another manipulation tactic used as a way to maintain power or control in a relationship.

Narcissists will use blame-shifting as a pattern of behavior that doesn't typically ease up. It allows them to avoid virtually all accountability for their actions and behaviors. This tactic will also exhaust you because a narcissist will continue arguing their points of blame towards you until you have no choice but to give up.

Blame-shifting is used in order to literally make you feel bad for getting into an argument with the narcissist in the first place. There are 17 typical blame-shifting phrases a narcissist will use in an argument.

1. **"Why are you always so mean and critical of me?"**

   Because the narcissist wants to make you forget their wrongdoings and the things you were actually fighting over, they use this phrase to turn the blame around on you by accusing you of being too critical. This is their way to redirect the argument, so once again, it's all your fault. THey paint you as the bully and the bad guy. If you are forced to truly ask yourself if you're being unfair, it lets them off the hook.

2. **"It's always your fault."**

This is only from the narcissist's point of view. Take a quick look at the actual facts, and you will understand how untrue this phrase is.

3. **"You're too soft-hearted and easily hurt."**

A narcissist uses this phrase to belittle you. They also use it when the narcissist has done something they know is hurtful, but they are trying to blame someone else instead of taking responsibility. This phrase can make it seem like you are the one who is being unreasonable. This is one of the manipulative phrases a narcissist uses that makes it harder for you to defend yourself because it can leave you questioning yourself.

4. **"I'm not arguing; I'm just discussing."**

When a narcissist says this, it's a form of deflection and manipulation. They're seeking to disarm you and establish an upper hand in the conversation, suggesting that any perceived conflict or confrontation is your fault, not theirs.

By framing their aggressive or provocative statements as mere "discussion," they attempt to normalize their behavior and diminish your emotional responses. This tactic can make you second-guess your own reactions, causing self-doubt and confusion to creep into your thinking. This phrase effectively reframes the narcissist as a rational, calm participant while painting you as overly emotional or reactive, thereby tilting the power balance in their favor.

5. **"If you wouldn't piss me off, I wouldn't have to say mean things to you."**

Consider this: how often has the narcissist angered you. Did it ever provoke you into using harsh or hurtful words like they do? It's unlikely. That speaks volumes. Regardless of how upset you may become, resorting to offensive and harmful responses is never justified. This phrase, "If you wouldn't piss me off, I wouldn't have to say mean things to you," is nothing but a blatant attempt to justify their abusive behavior and evade responsibility. It's crucial to remember that there's no excuse for such conduct, and it's absolutely not your fault.

6. **"You are always looking for something to complain about."**

With this phrase, the narcissist cleverly deflects blame, ensuring the finger always points at you and never at them. It's essential not to fall for this ruse, mistakenly believing every disagreement or issue stems from your actions. The narcissist's tactic is a mere sidestep from acknowledging their own role in the argument or conflict.

7. **"It's not my fault - you made me do it."**

This phrase is a classic illustration of a narcissist's avoidance of personal responsibility. Asserting that their poor behavior or uncontrollable outbursts are your doing, they attempt to pass the blame onto you. But bear in mind, it's never within your power to coerce a narcissist into any action they don't willingly choose. This pattern of blaming is their coping mechanism since they rarely, if ever, see themselves as the origin of the problem.

8. **"It would help if you spent less time with other people."**

Understand that this phrase is a classic deflection tactic used by a narcissist to evade responsibility for their actions, particularly when they've treated you poorly or even resorted to yelling. In this manner, they wrongfully assign you the blame because, in their distorted viewpoint, they are never at fault. Always remember, there's no circumstance where you can force or control a narcissist's actions against their will. The responsibility for their behavior squarely lies on their shoulders.

9. **"You need to learn to communicate better."**

When a narcissist uses this phrase, they are skilfully shifting blame onto you. They are suggesting that the true problem lies in your communication abilities, not their own mistakes. This subtle tactic can cause you to question your ability to express yourself and subtly undermines your confidence. Essentially, it's a deflection strategy designed to escape their own shortcomings and responsibilities. By accusing you of poor communication, they distract from the real issue - their own problematic behavior. This helps maintain the power dynamics in their favor in the relationship, escalating their control.

10. "It's your fault that I feel this way."

This phrase is a key example of blame shifting and avoiding personal responsibility. When a narcissist utters these words, they are essentially trying to manipulate you into taking responsibility for their feelings. They ignore the fact that feelings are a personal response to situations or circumstances. While it's true that your actions can elicit an emotional response from someone, how a person manages, expresses, and reacts to their emotions is entirely their responsibility. A narcissist, however, will attempt to distort this reality to avoid any sense of personal accountability and maintain their self-perceived superiority. This statement showcases their inability to reflect on their reactions or to take ownership of their emotions, which is a fundamental part of emotional maturity.

11. "You are so self-centered."

This phrase can be particularly harmful coming from a narcissist. The accusation of being self-centered seeks to turn the tables, implying that you are the one who is selfish and neglectful of others' needs. This is far from the truth, but the narcissist employs this tactic to shift focus from their own self-centered behavior. Typically, this phrase might be used when the narcissist is not getting what they want, and they want to manipulate you into feeling guilty for not acquiescing to their demands. This unjust accusation is just another attempt to control and manipulate you, by painting you as the person in the wrong. It's vital to recognize this for what it is - a deflection and projection of their own narcissistic tendencies.

12. "I can't believe you are even saying this."

This phrase is another tool in the narcissist's arsenal, designed to make you question your own judgment and feelings. Chances are, your words or assertions aren't inherently wrong or harmful. However, by expressing disbelief or shock, the narcissist aims to shift all responsibility onto you, making you the perceived wrongdoer. This tactic serves to undermine your confidence and sense of reality, furthering the narcissist's control and shifting focus away from their own behavior. Remember, this is a manipulative strategy, not a reflection of the validity of your words or feelings.

13. "You did this yourself - it's your fault."

This statement is a typical narcissistic tactic to deflect blame and shirk responsibility for any negative outcomes. By claiming that you're the sole architect of the issue, the narcissist can neatly sidestep their own involvement or wrongdoing. This phrase also serves to instill guilt, creating a sense that you must have committed some error to deserve the current unpleasant circumstances. Keep in mind that this is a manipulative strategy designed to control and confuse, not a fair assessment of the situation or your role in it.

14. "Why can't you be more like them?"

This statement epitomizes a common narcissistic tactic: the harmful practice of comparison. Narcissists often use this technique to exert control and maintain a power imbalance. By unfavorably contrasting you with others, they aim to dent your self-esteem and make you question your worth. This behavior can severely impact your mental health, making you feel as though you need to change to earn their approval. Remember, the narcissist's tendency to make such comparisons often stems from their own lack of self-worth. They project their insecurities onto others, failing to see the unique value of the individual before them.

15. "You're the one with the problem - not me."
When a narcissist employs this phrase, they are using a classic deflection tactic. By shifting the blame and fault onto you, they dodge accountability for their own actions and behaviors. This maneuver allows them to avoid introspection and personal growth, effectively preserving their skewed self-perception of perfection. In reality, the significant problem at hand is not you but the narcissist's inability to acknowledge their own shortcomings or errors. It's important to remember that their habit of blame-shifting is a manifestation of their disorder, and it doesn't reflect on your character or worth. Their inability to take responsibility doesn't mean you are at fault; it signifies their struggle with vulnerability and authentic self-awareness.

16. "It's not my fault - it's because of money/stress/you/work/etc."
A narcissist carries an innate sense of victimhood, according to research, which is

why they are quick to shift the blame over to you, or even another external factor in which they have little control over. Two classic blame-shifting strategies a narcissist uses include playing the victim card and becoming defensive. By using this phrase, a narcissist actually is saying that taking any accountability for their actions would require them to shed their ego, and they are incapable of doing that.

17. "You are overreacting."

A narcissist fundamentally believes that you are the source of all issues in the relationship. In their eyes, they never do anything wrong. Instead of acknowledging their mistakes and taking responsibility for their actions or behaviors, they find it easier to dismiss you as "overreacting". This tactic serves as a convenient escape route from accountability.

18. "What about the time you…"

Whataboutisms are the act or practice of responding to an accusation of wrongdoing by claiming that an offense committed by another is similar or worse. It's a conversational tactic in which the narcissist responds to an argument or attack by changing the subject to focus on someone else's misconduct, implying that all criticism is invalid because no one is completely blameless.

Excusing your mistakes with whataboutism is not the same as defending your actions, but it's a great way to muddy the waters and confound you long enough to take the focus away from them.

19. "You like being the victim."

This is a classic manipulative tactic, designed to divert the blame and make you question your own feelings and sanity.

⚜ *After months of feeling disrespected and dismissed by a guy I was seeing, I finally found the courage to voice my feelings. We sat down one evening, and I started sharing my experiences, my frustrations, my fears. I was nervous, but I thought if I spoke calmly and rationally, he would understand and things would change.*

But instead of acknowledging my concerns, he reacted in the most unexpected way. He smirked and said, "You like being the victim, don't you?" His words hit me like a punch to the gut. Was he implying that my feelings of pain were nothing more than me wanting to play the victim?

His accusation left me feeling stunned and ridiculed. It was as if my legitimate feelings were nothing more than a melodramatic performance in his eyes. The worst part was that, for a moment, I questioned myself, wondering if I really was overreacting, and that maybe I was just playing the victim.

Chapter 5: 19 Gaslighting Phrases

⚜ *Each time I'd consider leaving my wife, she'd throw in, "You're lucky to have me." It was her way of undermining my self-worth, and making me feel like no one else would ever want me. It was a shitty manipulation tactic,and looking back at how beaten up and dominated I felt all the time, I understand why I fell for it, even though I'm not proud of it.*

Narcissistic gaslighting is a destructive form of emotional abuse aimed at distorting truth, isolating victims, and fostering self-doubt. Narcissists are experts at making you question your memories, perceptions, and judgment. They will deny your experiences, manipulate your reality, and even play the victim to deflect responsibility.

Charming on the surface but manipulative at their core, narcissists excel at making you feel guilty, overly sensitive, and inadequate. They thrive on deception and evasion, blaming you for their faults while cleverly eluding responsibility. Their objective: bolster their ego, assert control, and mask their insecurities.

After a spin with such artfully deceptive behavior, you'll be left with a dizzying sense of feeling disoriented, powerless, and alone, impacting your emotional health and social functioning. This chapter shines the spotlight on 19 common gaslighting phrases narcissists use to manipulate and control you during conflicts.

1. **"You will never have the confidence to leave me!"**

   A narcissist already knows about your low self-esteem issues, particularly if you have never had the guts to stand up for yourself and have always sought validation from the narcissist. They may actually believe that you won't have the guts to leave them, no matter how badly they mistreat you, but they use this phrase as a way to hurt you even more by further damaging your self-esteem.

2. **"Don't blame me, I never meant to hurt you."**

   Upon hearing this phrase, expect the conversation to come to a sudden standstill. This statement operates as a smokescreen, designed to divert attention away from their damaging behavior. They deploy it as a tool to absolve themselves of the repercussions of their actions. Moreover, after dropping this line, a narcissist often resorts to the silent treatment. This punitive measure further removes them from accountability, serving as a manipulative tactic to control the narrative and the emotional dynamics of the interaction. It's their way of shifting the responsibility onto you, avoiding the need to face the harmful impact of their actions.

3. "No wonder nobody likes you."

This phrase is a typical manipulation tactic narcissists use to chip away at your self-esteem and breed a sense of isolation. By insisting that no one else could possibly value or love you as they do, they aim to plant seeds of insecurity and dependence. It's paramount not to believe such distortions! In reality, there are numerous people in your life who genuinely care for you and stand ready to support you in all situations. Narcissists wield this strategy knowing that the more isolated and estranged you feel, the less likely you are to extract yourself from their control.

4. "You're not making any sense."

When a narcissist tells you this, they're essentially attempting to discredit your thoughts and experiences, and undermine your mental acuity. Their intent is to depict your reactions or feelings as illogical or unfounded, even when they're entirely justified. Through this, they aspire to control the conversation and make you question your own mental stability and discernment.

Moreover, this phrase is a classic form of deflection that aids the narcissist in shirking responsibility for their actions or behaviors.

Instead of owning up to their faults or transgressions, they turn the focus onto your supposed inability to reason or communicate effectively. This tactic is designed to keep you on the back foot, which ultimately makes it easier for them to manipulate and dominate the dynamics of the relationship."

5. **"We've already talked about this, don't you remember?"**

When a narcissist says this, they're implementing a calculated strategy for manipulation within their gaslighting tactics. The objective is to instill doubt in your memory, fostering feelings of uncertainty and disorientation. By asserting that a past discussion or arrangement occurred — when in fact it didn't — they aim to shake your confidence in your own recall, evade accountability for unresolved matters, and heighten their control in the relationship.

This form of psychological manipulation is a signature trait of narcissistic abuse, designed to erode your self-assurance and amplify their power over you. Over time, this tactic can make you increasingly dependent on the narcissist's version of reality, further cementing their control."

6. **"Why are you making this up?"**

The assertion, "You are making this up," is a classic gaslighting tactic often utilized by narcissists. Its purpose isn't to foster resolution or mutual understanding, but to dismiss your feelings and experiences as mere fabrications. In confrontations involving a narcissist, the objective is seldom about achieving reconciliation but more about asserting dominance.

By insinuating that you're creating issues or conflicts out of thin air, they aim to sow seeds of doubt regarding your perceptions and memories. This approach facilitates the continuation of their abusive behavior unopposed, as over time it erodes your ability to trust your own experiences or confront their malpractices confidently. This tactic of denial and invalidation forms a crucial part of the manipulative arsenal employed by narcissists to maintain control in their relationships.

7. **"Stop imagining things."**

The statement, "Stop imagining things," is a direct attack on your perceptions and reality, and it's a typical example of a gaslighting tactic used by narcissists. By challenging your sense of reality, this statement can make you feel like you're losing your mental grasp, thereby undermining your confidence in your own experiences, opinions, and beliefs.

From the narcissist's viewpoint, it's a strategic tool to maintain control and dominance over you. This happens because it weakens your ability to effectively challenge or question their actions or behavior. Among the various gaslighting tactics, this one particularly stands out due to its capability to inflict significant psychological damage.

8. **"You are overthinking it."**

This is commonly utilized by narcissists as a method to evade further discussion or confrontation about a concerning matter. It allows them to sidestep accountability for their abusive or inappropriate actions by suggesting that you're exaggerating the issue or attributing unnecessary complexity to it.

Especially if you're a person who tends to overthink, a narcissist might use this tactic to manipulate you into second-guessing your perceptions and responses. By doing so, they hope to instill the idea that you're making more out of the situation than it warrants. In reality, your concerns are most likely valid; the narcissist just wishes to avoid accepting their faults or facing the consequences of their behavior.

9. **"You're a bad person."**

You are an exceptional individual, far from the negative portrayal the narcissist attempts to project onto you. You are simply someone who innocently developed feelings for a narcissistic individual.

10. "You're so insecure and jealous."

The narcissist aims to undermine your confidence by labeling you as insecure and jealous. This tactic serves as a diversion from the real issue at hand. By confronting them with your doubts or presenting evidence of possible infidelity, you have struck a nerve, causing the narcissist to deflect blame onto you. Sadly, repeated exposure to this manipulation can lead to self-doubt and self-loathing. The narcissist finds solace in shifting focus away from their own self-hatred by making you feel inadequate instead. However, it is crucial to recognize that it is the narcissist who is truly insecure and afraid of losing you. They are projecting their own insecurities and jealousy onto you.

11. "Stop exaggerating."

The narcissist employs this phrase as a means to dismiss your grievances. They insinuate that you are embellishing or over-dramatizing your concerns, suggesting that they hold little importance. Instead of attentively listening to your worries, they choose to accuse you of exaggeration.

12. "You need to toughen up."

The narcissist employs this phrase in order to evade accountability for their actions. By presenting their behavior as "honesty" and suggesting that you need to accept the truth, they aim to absolve themselves of any responsibility. They try to convince you that your sensitivity is excessive, leading you to believe that you are fabricating issues or imagining problems that do not exist. However, this is far from the truth. Regardless of the extent of the narcissist's abuse and manipulation, they consistently shift the blame back to you, implying that you are weak or incapable of handling their actions.

13. "I'm not trying to control you. You are thinking about your ex-husband, and taking it out on me instead."

This statement is yet another manipulative tactic to deflect blame onto you and make you feel guilty. It is highly likely that you haven't even mentioned your ex-husband during the conversation, yet the narcissist brings him up to redirect the focus of the discussion. By doing so, they attempt to make you doubt yourself and question whether you are unfairly projecting your feelings onto them. However, it is important to recognize that this is a baseless accusation designed to manipulate your emotions and avoid taking responsibility for their own controlling behavior.

14. "You are so childish/immature."

The narcissist resorts to phrases like this in an attempt to belittle and undermine you. However, it is important to remember that their words do not define your true character. You are aware that this accusation is unfounded and simply untrue. In reality, it is often the narcissist themselves who engage in childish or immature behavior, as they tend to project their own flaws onto others. So, it is crucial not to internalize their attempts to make you feel bad about yourself, as their words are a reflection of their own issues, not yours.

15. "Listen to yourself! You're losing it!"

When the narcissist says this, they are attempting to discredit your valid expression of boundaries or assertiveness. They aim to undermine your confidence by suggesting that your reaction is irrational or unhinged. However, this is far from the truth. By standing up for yourself and refusing to tolerate their abusive and manipulative behavior, you are actually displaying a healthy and normal response. It is a sign of personal growth and self-preservation, showing that you are no longer willing to be subjected to their mistreatment. Do not let their false accusations diminish the progress you have made in asserting your own well-being.

16. "You don't even know what you are talking about."

This statement is a prime example of a narcissist's favored tactic known as gaslighting. This manipulation technique is employed to make you doubt your own reality and sanity. The narcissist, despite projecting confidence, is deeply insecure. Their inflated ego serves as a defense mechanism against perceived threats, including any form of criticism. When confronted with a differing opinion or challenge, the narcissist becomes defensive and attempts to assert superiority. By asserting that you lack understanding or knowledge, they aim to devalue and diminish your perspective. Ultimately, this statement is a reflection of their own insecurity and their inclination to devalue you when they feel threatened.

17. "You need help."

When the narcissist states "You need help," it is important not to internalize their words. Remember that it is not you who requires help, but rather the narcissist themselves. They are projecting their anger onto you and attempting to manipulate you into believing their false claims. It is crucial to recognize their behavior as a reflection of their own issues and not let their words undermine your self-worth.

18. "You aren't perfect either."

This remark is a strategic maneuver to divert attention away from their own wrongdoing and redirect the conversation. By bringing up past mistakes or flaws, they aim to shift the focus away from the current issue you are trying to address. Their intention is to put you on the defensive and prevent a meaningful discussion about their behavior. It is essential to recognize this tactic and stay focused on addressing the specific concern at hand, rather than allowing them to sidetrack the conversation.

19. "You're nothing without me."

When a narcissist says, "You're nothing without me," it is an attempt to assert their dominance and control over you. They harbor an exaggerated belief in their own power and accomplishments, considering themselves superior to others. Consequently, they become angered when they do not receive the admiration and recognition they believe they deserve. As part of their mocking and demeaning behavior, narcissists may even attempt to take credit for your achievements. They aim to make you feel indebted to them for your success, implying that you owe your accomplishments to their involvement. In reality, their statement reflects their desire to share in your glory to maintain their narcissistic supply and validate their inflated ego.

⚜ *My ex-boyfriend was a master of gaslighting. I remember how, during almost every disagreement we had, he would spin a web of lies and distortions that would leave me questioning my own reality. This was his way of maintaining control, and unfortunately, it worked.*

An example of this would be when he hurt my feelings. It didn't matter what the offense was - a thoughtless comment, a harsh tone, a neglectful act. Whenever I tried to confront him about it, instead of acknowledging his actions or expressing any form of remorse, he would turn it back on me. He'd insist that I was misunderstanding him, that I was imagining things or even making things up.

In his eyes, my feelings were never valid. It was as if he held the monopoly on reality and only his version of events held any truth. Time and again, he would shift blame onto me, and because I was caught in his manipulative hold, I'd start to doubt my memory and judgment.

I recall feeling so frustrated and stupid trying to explain how his actions upset me. Eventually, I stopped voicing my feelings completely. But that only resulted in a buildup of silent resentment, turning me into a ticking time bomb that was detrimental to my emotional health.

Looking back now, I can see clearly the destructive dynamics of our relationship and how his gaslighting made me doubt my reality, suppress my feelings, and hold onto grudges. It's a bitter memory, but an important lesson about the signs of emotional manipulation. If my story can help someone else, and I hope it can, I don't mind reliving this terrible time in my life for the benefit of others.

Chapter 6: Mic Drop: 20 Phrases to End an Argument With a Narcissist

Engaging in a dispute with a narcissist is challenging due to their propensity to disregard the rules of fair play. The emotionally charged and damaging nature of these conflicts can even compromise your mental well-being.

Some individuals may try to bring an end to these disputes by sidestepping the narcissist or entirely withdrawing from the argument. Others might attempt to confront the narcissist and calm the storm. This can indeed be a daunting task, yet it can be achieved given ample patience and time.

So, how do you genuinely bring closure to a disagreement with a narcissist? Is it a feasible task? In response to your queries, there exist several dependable phrases that can either entirely disarm a narcissist or soothe the volatility of a heated dispute. We'll explore some of the most effective and commonly used phrases to conclude a disagreement with a narcissist in the subsequent sections.

1. **"I hear what you are saying."**
   Each narcissist craves validation and being heard, making this phrase a swift

antidote to a heated argument. You are affirming that you comprehend the narcissist's viewpoint. You are not obligated to concur with their sentiment. In numerous instances, just the act of acknowledging their standpoint can diffuse the argument. The narcissist, usually feeling recognized, will likely simmer down, and may even opt to bring closure to the dispute independently.

2. **"I see where you are coming from."**
   While you may not align with the narcissist's reasoning, using this phrase allows them to feel as though their line of thought has validity. It acknowledges their perspective without necessarily agreeing with it, lending them a sense of being understood.

3. **"I cannot control how you feel about me."**
   This statement serves as a reminder that you are the only one who has control over your own emotions and actions. The narcissist must understand that their emotional reactions cannot dictate your conduct. Moreover, it signals to the narcissist that their skewed perceptions won't sway your behavior or sense of self.

4. **"Your perspective is interesting."**
   This statement neither affirms nor disputes the narcissist's assertions, giving the

impression that all viewpoints are valued, irrespective of their validity. It grants the narcissist space to reflect on their emotions, creating an opportunity for a pause in the argument. This break can be effectively used to introduce another phrase to further defuse the tension.

5. **"I am not going to argue anymore."**
To make this effective, you need to adhere to your word and physically disengage. This sends a clear message that you're choosing to withdraw from an argument that isn't leading anywhere productive.

6. **"Let's agree to disagree."**
This statement communicates that while you acknowledge their perspective, you are not willing to change your stance. But instead of engaging further, you're suggesting mutual respect and a cessation of the argument. Remember, it's less about winning with a narcissist and more about maintaining your own peace of mind.

7. **"I understand that you're disappointed and upset, and I am willing to listen to your feelings and thoughts."**
This sentence affirms their emotions while subtly encouraging open communication. However, it doesn't compromise your own

perspective. Offering a listening ear can help pacify the situation, but remember to maintain boundaries and not get sucked into their emotional turmoil.

8. **"Can we aim to be respectful in our conversation?"**

This question, although seemingly rhetorical, offers a potent pivot point, a moment to recalibrate the conversation's tone. It's a subtle reminder that emotional respect should be at the heart of your interactions, thus helping to diffuse a potentially explosive situation.

9. **"I want to share how I feel."**

This is a phrase that helps you assert your right to voice your emotions and perspectives when dealing with a narcissist. It's an attempt to refocus the conversation about your feelings - without blaming or accusing. It's about asserting *your* needs in the face of a narcissist's potential dismissiveness or control over the conversation. Just remember, though, it doesn't guarantee an empathetic response from the narcissist, but is a crucial step in setting boundaries.

10. **"Well, this is not going very well. I am quite sure we can do better. Let's start over, and try again."**

Utilizing this phrase acts as a strategic halt to a spiraling argument with a narcissist. It also serves as a means to postpone the debate until a time when emotions have simmered down. By suggesting a 'do-over', it conveys your commitment to resolving issues without the unnecessary drama.

11. "I'm sorry you feel that way."

Using this phrase allows you to express empathy for the narcissist's feelings without compromising on your personal boundaries. Maintaining boundaries when dealing with a narcissist is crucially important. This expression both acknowledges the narcissist's emotions and holds them accountable for their reactions. It also serves as an effective tool to prevent further escalation of the conflict.

12. "Your anger is not my responsibility."

This statement serves as a grounding principle, establishing an unmistakable boundary outlining what you are and aren't accountable for. It aids in resetting the dynamics of the conversation, making it clear that the narcissist cannot use you as their narcissistic supply to assuage their emotional turbulence.

13. "I don't like how you're talking to me, so I will not engage any longer."

This statement is arguably the most powerful tool for curtailing a narcissist and swiftly concluding an argument. It asserts your decision to reject toxic dialogue. You have the prerogative, at any moment, to decisively disengage from the argument, irrespective of their agreement. A narcissist thrives on provoking emotional reactions. With this phrase, you signal your withdrawal from the dispute, thereby effectively severing their source of satisfaction.

14. "We both have a right to our own opinions."

This statement underscores that the narcissist has a right to their viewpoint. Yet, you are simultaneously asserting that you understand their utterances are merely their opinions, not incontrovertible facts. A narcissist aspires to feel superior and maintain total control over the conversation. However, this remark makes it unambiguous that you won't let that transpire. You're not prepared to relinquish your own stance, but you also have no desire to perpetuate the argument. By invoking this phrase, you illustrate your capacity to respect their entitlement to their viewpoint, as is your right too. This should prompt them to discontinue the dispute, at least for the time being.

15. "I am capable of doing what I want, regardless of what you think."

This phrase makes it abundantly clear that you already have your perspective and they will not be able to change the way you feel. You are also making it clear that their opinion on the issue at hand is not going to shape your behaviors. You will show you strong self-esteem with this phrase, and actually resist the narcissistic abuse as well. You will show the narcissist that you are a strong individual and will not allow any other person to control or interfere in your life in any way.

16. "Your anger is not my fault. I refuse to take the blame for it."

This statement loudly communicates that you already possess your own viewpoint and it's impervious to any attempts at alteration. Further, you clarify that their stance on the matter at hand won't dictate your actions. The use of this phrase not only demonstrates your robust self-esteem but also offers a firm resistance against narcissistic manipulation. It conveys to the narcissist that you're a resilient individual who won't tolerate any form of control or interference in your life.

17. "I can work with this, but I draw the line to be insulted or yelled at."

This statement establishes your approach to engaging with a narcissist steeped in grandiosity. You express your willingness to participate in a healthy debate while simultaneously setting clear boundaries about unacceptable behavior.

18. "I understand."

This doesn't signify your agreement with their stance, just your understanding of it. Narcissists crave acknowledgment and validation, and by communicating your understanding, they are likely to feel less defensive. This can significantly contribute towards calming the argumentative atmosphere.

19. "Everything is okay."

This affirmation helps the narcissist to understand that they will eventually find stability, as tumultuous moments are transitory. Narcissists struggle with managing intense emotions or conflict due to a lack of self-awareness. This statement provides them the affirmation or reassurance they may subconsciously be seeking.

20. "I can accept how you feel."

Narcissists are notoriously unyielding in their views, making it futile to attempt to shift their perspective or alter their convictions.

Instead of engaging in a pointless argument, simply affirming that you acknowledge their feelings or opinions can effectively defuse the situation. By doing so, you deprive them of the argumentative engagement they seek, hence cutting off their supply.

Conclusion

Narcissists thrive on discord; that's the stark reality we've delved into throughout this journey. We've explored the underlying motives behind their fondness for conflict, and dissected 99 phrases they commonly employ during disagreements. This deep dive started with an examination of 21 manipulation tactics, and some proved to be particularly prevalent:

- "You have trust issues."
- "I love you more than anything."
- "You are too sensitive."
- "I'm only doing this because I love you."
- "I'm the best you'll ever have."
- "It's always something with you."

Moving into Chapter 2, we unpacked an array of 19 defensive statements commonly deployed by narcissists in the heat of disputes, such as:

- "You are overreacting."
- "I'm already going through so much - thanks for making it worse."
- "You are way too emotional."
- "I do so much for you."
- "How dare you accuse me of doing that!"

- "That never happened."

Advancing to Chapter 3, we delved into the frequent mocking remarks narcissists relish tossing about in disputes. A few of these are:

- "It was just a joke."
- "Here we go again."
- "I can't have any negative emotions around you."
- "Relax. It's not that big of a deal."
- "You're being irrational."
- "You're so lucky I put up with you."

Subsequently, in Chapter 4, we inspected 19 blame-shifting expressions habitually employed by narcissists amid quarrels. Some of the recurrently used blame-shifting phrases are:

- "You're too soft-hearted and easily hurt."
- "You are always looking for something to complain about."
- "It's not my fault - you made me do it."
- "You are so self-centered."
- "I can't believe you are even saying this."
- "You are the one with the problem - not me."

Finally in Chapter 5, we explored 19 frequently used gaslighting expressions favored by narcissists during confrontations. Among the commonly employed gaslighting phrases are:

- "You are not making any sense."
- "You are making this up."
- "We've already talked about this, don't you remember?"
- "Stop imagining things."
- "You are overthinking it."
- "Stop exaggerating."

Upon understanding the intricate web of phrases a narcissist spins during a dispute, we delved into Chapter 6, presenting you with 20 effective phrases to help you disengage from a confrontation with a narcissist. Some of the most powerful ones include:

- "I see where you are coming from."
- "Your perspective is interesting."
- "I am not going to argue anymore."
- "Let's agree to disagree.
- "I want to share how I feel.
- "I'm sorry you feel that way.

Encountering a narcissist in a confrontation is neither a pleasant nor an easy experience. Personally, I have navigated relationships with several narcissists and can attest to the turbulent storm that their argumentative nature brews. They are relentless, often unyielding even in the face of their glaring errors, and alarmingly, they have a knack for swaying you to their perspective even when you're consciously aware of its fallacy!

The ordeal is more than just exasperating. But armed with the insights from this book, you should now possess the resources to deftly put an end to a conflict with the narcissist in your life. If you've had interactions with a narcissist before, you likely found a familiar ring in the phrases we dissected. With your newfound understanding, you'll be better equipped to decipher their motivations behind each manipulative expression.

Other Books by Kristen Thrasher

Gaslighting and Narcissism Series:

1. Gaslighting in Relationships: Why Adults With ADHD are More Vulnerable to Gaslighting Specific Steps to Free Yourself From a Gaslit Relationship
2. Gaslighting Abuse: 66 Tips to Stop a Gaslighter, Including the Gray Rock Method
3. Co-Parenting With a Narcissistic Ex: Strategies For Parallel Parenting When Your Toxic Ex Has Narcissism
4. Narcissistic Relationships: Strategies to Emotionally Detach, Steps to End the Relationship, and Coping Mechanisms to Help You Stay Away
5. Gaslighting and Narcissism 4 Book Series: Gaslighting in Relationships, Gaslighting Abuse, Narcissistic Relationships, and Co-Parenting With a Narcissistic Ex
6. 75 Co-Parenting Hacks: Strategies to Co-Parent With a Narcissist, Improve Your Relationship With Your Ex, Overcome Conflict, and Better Yourself

ADHD Series:

1. Moms With ADHD: Strategies for Women Parenting With Adult ADHD
2. 87 Tips and Tricks for Women With ADHD: Survive the Chaos of Living With Adult ADHD, Manage Your Symptoms, and Live Your Best Life

3. 301 Positive Affirmations for Adults Suffering With ADHD: For Women, Men, and Teens: Learn to Manage Your Impulsiveness, Hyperactivity, Irritability, Time Management, Disorganization, and More
4. ADHD in Adults: 2 Part Series: 87 Tips and Tricks for Women With ADHD and 301 Positive Affirmations for Adults Suffering With ADHD
5. Understanding ADHD in Women: Strategies for Women Diagnosed With ADHD in Adulthood: Manage Your Symptoms as An Adult Living With Attention Deficit Hyperactivity Disorder
6. How ADHD Affects Relationships
7. Relationship Series: Gaslighting in Relationships and How ADHD Affects Relationships
8. ADHD Time Blindness: 27 Hacks to Combat Time Blindness
9. Stop Procrastinating: 47 Hacks to Get Your Ass in Gear
10. Impulsive ADHD: 97 Hacks to Manage Impulsivity
11. 171 ADHD Life Hacks: Impulsivity, Procrastinating, and Time Blindness

Eating Disorder Series:
1. Eating Disorders in Children and Teens: A Comprehensive Parent's Guide to Eating Disorder Recovery

2. Understanding Body Dysmorphic Disorder: Causes, Treatment, Self-Care Tips, and Supporting Your Loved One

Parenting Series:
1. Parenting the ADHD Child: 113 Tips and Tricks for Raising a Child With ADHD
2. Parenting the SPD Child: Strategies for Raising a Child With Sensory Processing Disorder
3. Parenting the Autistic Child: 161 Tips and Tricks for Raising a Child on the Autism Spectrum
4. Parenting the Special Needs Child: 124 Tips and Tricks for Parenting a Child With a Disability
5. 4 Book Parenting Series: Parenting the SPD Child, Parenting the ADHD Child, Parenting the Autistic Child, and Parenting the Special Needs Child

Positive Affirmations Series:
1. 409 Positive Affirmations for Recovering From an Eating Disorder
2. 365 Positive Affirmations While Facing a Divorce
3. Positive Affirmations: 3 Book Series Including Divorce, Eating Disorders, and ADHD
4. Positive Self-Love Affirmations

Animal Trivia for Kids Series
1. Horse Trivia: Fun Facts About Horses for Kids

2. Dolphin Trivia: Fun Facts About Dolphins for Kids
3. Animal Trivia for Kids Part 1: Horses and Dolphins
4. Cat Trivia: Fun Facts About Cats for Kids
5. Dog Trivia: Fun Facts About Dogs for Kids
6. Ape and Monkey Trivia: Fun Facts About Apes and Monkeys for Kids
7. Alligator and Crocodile Trivia: Fun Facts About Apes and Monkeys and Alligators and Crocodiles for Kids

Stand-Alone Titles:
1. The Unofficial Friends TV Show Book: The One With all the Quotes
2. Bipolar Disorder Hacks: 47 Tips and Tricks, Self-Management Strategies, and Ways to Cope

Made in the USA
Monee, IL
29 August 2024

83bd40a3-9c22-44ee-819f-d9e1c7813f02R01